DOG WALKS
North Scotland

TRACEY MILLIER RADNALL

The author has made every effort to ensure that the information in this
publication is accurate, and accepts no responsibility whatsoever for any loss,
injury or inconvenience experienced by any person or persons using this book.

Published by
Tracey Millier Radnall
wildtimes.co.uk
Copyright ©Tracey Millier Radnall 2021

Design, illustration and photography ©Tracey Millier Radnall
Cover photography: Tracey Millier Radnall

ISBN 978-0-9930157-2-4
A catalogue record for this book is available from the British Library

Printed by Cambrian Printers Ltd, Wales

MIX
Paper from
responsible sources
FSC® C004116
FSC
www.fsc.org

Loch Maree and Slioch
from Slattadale Forest

Hebrides

Off The Beaten Track

WALK RATING

The more dark paws
= the harder the route

One Paw: Gentle stroll,
mostly short and flat,
suitable for all fitness levels

Two Paws: Moderate,
undulating longer walks

Three Paws: Hilly, requires
reasonable fitness and good
walking boots and clothing

Four Paws: Long walks with
hilly, rough terrain. Good
outdoor equipment and
boots, water & food needed.
Dog harness, compass and
GPS device advised

WALK TYPES

- ● COASTAL & WATER
- ● FOREST & WOODLAND
- ● HILLS & MOUNTAINS
- ● CASTLES & MONUMENTS
- ● NATIONAL PARKS & TRAILS

MAP SYMBOLS

- ✪ POINT OF INTEREST
- ♆ LIGHTHOUSE
- 🌳 FOREST
- ⚓ HARBOUR
- 🏰 CASTLE OR FORT
- 🏚 CABIN OR BOTHY
- ▲ PEAK
- ⛺ CAMPING
- Ⓥ VISITOR CENTRE
- ✺ BEACH & STARFISH
- 🐦 WILD FOWL
- ⛏ CAVE OR CAIRN

The Spaniel route

Welcome to the pack

From the whisky trails of Moray and the lofty Cairngorms to the unique rocky routes of Sutherland and island hopping among remote sandy beaches – there are a huge variety of adventures to be had in North Scotland.

6,000 miles of coastline – 10,000 including the strings of islands – plus more than 30,000 lochs… Scotland is the perfect adventure. You and your dog will love exploring the diverse landscape bound by some of the rarest rocks in the world. There is so much to see and do, so take your time! The sunniest place in Scotland is East Lothian and, of course, the west benefits from the Gulf Stream, meaning you'll find starfish and palm trees on the isle coasts.

The walks

In this book you'll find a variety of walks and adventures across North Scotland, including local information and maps plus places to stay and eat. Many of the walks are rich in history, unique sites of interest and wildlife – and ALL with fantastic views.

Thanks...

…To the many furry friends and their folks who have joined me on the walks in this book. Domino, Milly, Elvis, Bertie, a tale of two Charlies, Bonn, Bob, Hattie, Biscuit, Percy and Snowy. Thanks to their canine-loving humans too – Louise, Mitch, Jonny, 'Fingers' Feely, Jules, 'Bulldog' Drummond, Eva and Sandy.

I couldn't conclude without mentioning my best pal – Bertie, a Working Cocker Spaniel. Without his epicness and enduring enthusiasm, this book would never have been made. He has been my companion on most of these walks, and is a regular reviewer for *Dog Friendly Magazine*. Someone asked me once while compiling a review: "Does he work?" "Oh yes," I replied. "He's my wing-man and model." Not only is he a seasoned pro in front of the camera, he is constantly keen as mustard, happy and handsome.

As soon as I reach for a rucksack Bertie jumps to a new level of alertness. He not only hides inside the overnight bag, but also stuffs his favourite ball (or whatever is handy) in there with him – refusing to move until said bag is transported to the car.

We are based in East Lothian, the heart of John Muir country. As the ground-breaking man once said: "Walking is commensurate with thinking," and we've done a lot of that while compiling this book during this exceptional year of lockdown. I hope you enjoy visiting many of the places in the book – I would love to hear your tales (wildtimes.co.uk) ●

The author & Bertie on Elgol, Isle of Skye (left). Above: Charlie, Ralph, Milly, Elvis, Bonn and co with their humans

Top Travel Tips

Travelling to North Scotland can take a little more planning, especially with one or more dogs in tow. Here, Tracey Radnall gives some handy safety and comfort tips to ensure you all arrive in style.

Stay safe on the move

Many dogs like to move freely in the back of the car, and having a crate or dog-guard (padded with their own bedding and toys) will make the journey safer for both you and them. It will stop them from distracting you and, in the event of an accident, your pet will be less likely to escape. Other useful restraint options, such as seatbelt harnesses, are ideal too – simply choose the option that is best for the size of your car and the number of dogs travelling.

Take regular breaks

Long car journeys can be tiring for dogs and, just like you, they need to stop for a regular comfort break. Most dogs will appreciate the opportunity for a little stroll and a few sniffs, and Scotland is blessed with roadside open spaces and forestry areas across the country. These offer ideal space away from the main roads and many have toilet blocks, picnic areas and paths for a longer walk too. I have included a few routes close to major trunk roads.

Keep your cool

The sun is very intense in Scotland from April to September and can be misleading, even when the ambient air temperature may seem cool. It's worth bearing in mind that the day length in Scotland is also much longer in summer, reaching 18 hours of daylight by mid-June.

Stock up on water

Fresh water is essential on long journeys. I always pack a collapsible bowl for the trip and keep bottled water handy at all times, especially if wild camping. Scotland is blessed with fresh water sources, and a carbon water filter bottle is a good addition when camping in summer or staying in a bothy, where there may not be fresh running water.

Food for thought

Your dog is bound to be excited, so have a few treats to hand to reward them for being good. Your dog is probably used to a routine at home, including set feeding and walkie times. It's best to maintain this routine to make them feel as comfortable as possible on holiday. Make sure that you take enough of your dog's regular food in case you can't find it locally - a holiday isn't the best time to start new food! Also take your dog's bed, blanket and toys; the more things they have from home, the more likely they are to settle. I always pack my digital radio or USB speaker to play our favourite radio stations and music in a new place. Often, holiday cottages in Scotland have a poor mobile signal so having your own entertainment is a good idea.

Insurance & chips

If anything should happen while you're away, you need to be prepared. Having pet insurance is the best way to make sure you're covered (remember to take a copy of the policy with you). Microchip providers will allow you to register temporary addresses, and always keep your mobile number up-to-date on the data records.

Fuelling & charging

It's best to keep topped up with car fuel when in Scotland, especially when visiting more remote areas. Electric charge places are now widespread across Scotland, even in many small villages. For a live map of charge places see the link below. *chargeplacesscotland.org/live-map*

GLOSSARY

Common Gaelic language used in local signage, text and OS maps:

abhainn river
ailean field, grassy plain
àirigh shilling, hill pasture
allt burn, stream
àth ford

bàn white
beag small
bealach pass, gorge
beinn ben, hill
bràighe upper part

ceum path
cìoch pointed rock
clach boulder, stone
cnoc hillock
coire corrie, cauldron, hollow
creachann exposed rocky summit
creag cliff
cruach heap, stack

dubh black, dark

garbh thick, coarse, rough

lagan hollow, dimple
learg hillside exposed to sea or sun
lochan small loch, pool

machair fertile, low lying grassy plain
meall mound
mór big, tall

sgòrr peak, sharp point
sgùrr large conical hill
stùc pinnacle, precipice steep rock

➤

Ceum Path
Drochaid an Airgid
Silverbridge 1.5 km

CANINE KIT

Crash the biscuits!

deuter

28
ACT TRAIL
SL

> A comfy rucksack to carry extra layers, leads water, harness & treats

SNOWY'S HUMAN IS ORGANISED

Get your human to carry your favourite treats in a daysack

GEAR & KIT

Having the right practical dog accessories makes for a safe and comfortable trip for you and your hound. Here are a few recommended go-to pieces of kit…

Mountain Paws Dog Hiking Harness

An ideal lightweight harness, made using breathable and flexible fabric. Easy to adjust to fit, it works by slipping over the dog's head and clipping the adjustable straps under the front and rear torso. Very practical too with a padded top-mounted handle and alloy D-ring lead hook. Reflective detailing for visibility. **Verdict:** A useful piece of outdoor kit, ideal for busy and young dogs. Optional shock absorber lead available too.
mountainpaws.co.uk

DESIGN 10/10 FEATURES 10/10 USABILITY 10/10

DESIGN 10/10 FEATURES 10/10 USABILITY 10/10

Ruff & Tumble Drying Coat

A gorgeous towel drying coat that comes in a range of colours. This one is part of the Design Collection, complete with contemporary stripes. With double fabric thickness the quality is first rate. It's cotton, although feels like velvet, finished with cotton drill taped seems and fully adjustable Velcro fastenings. **Verdict:** A handy dog accessory while travelling or wild camping if your dog loves bounding around in the wet and muddy stuff.
ruffandtumbledogcoats.com

Pawfit 2 Pet Tracker

This smart pet location and activity tracking device attaches to your dog's collar, sending real-time information back to your smartphone as to your dog's whereabouts. Waterproof, with a long battery life, it records the distance your dog has covered. A subscription is needed to activate live tracking. **Verdict:** Excellent app and interface, with a long battery life. Active alert should anyone interfere with the device.
pawfit.com

DESIGN 10/10 FEATURES 10/10 USABILITY 9/10

Fido Pro Airlift

This is one of those useful pieces of kit to keep in your rucksack in the hope you will never need to use it. Designed in Colorado, this lightweight sling is a very handy way of carrying your dog if injured. It works by laying the Airlift on the ground with four holes for the legs. Place your dog over the four slots and lift the harness to cradle them. Carry the dog as if a rucksack.

Recommended by vets and mountain rescue teams. **Verdict:** Adventure with added piece of mind.
fidoprotection.com

DESIGN 10/10 FEATURES 9/10 USABILITY 9/10

Know the Code before you go

The Land Reform Act (2003) gives everyone rights of access over unenclosed land and inland water throughout Scotland, as long as they behave responsibly.

When outdoors you must follow the Scottish Outdoor Access Code. Scottish access rights apply to hills and moors, forests, woods, beaches, rivers and lochs: sometimes referred to as 'freedom to roam'.

Access rights apply to people walking dogs as long as their dogs are kept under close control. Activities also include walking, cycling, climbing, horse riding, kayaking, swimming and watching wildlife, but don't include shooting, fishing or access with motor vehicles. There are commonsense exceptions, including private houses and gardens, their yards, outbuildings or compounds.

The Scottish Outdoor Access Code is based on three key principles:
• Respect the interests of others.
• Care for the environment.
• Take responsibility for yourself.

Enjoying the outdoors responsibly
• Take responsibility for your own actions. This means your personal safety, so keep alert for hazards and take special care with dogs and children.
• Take care near livestock; keep your dog under control and always pick up after your dog.
• Respect people's privacy and peace of mind. Do not act in ways that might annoy or alarm people, especially at night.
• Keep clear of land management operations, such as harvesting and tree-felling, and leave gates as you find them.

Livestock
• Never let your dog worry farm animals or wildlife.
• Don't take your dog into fields

where there are lambs or calves.
• If you go into a field of farm animals, keep your dog on a short lead or close at heel.
• If cattle react aggressively and move towards you, keep calm, let your dog go and take the shortest, safest route out of the field.

Crops
• Don't take your dog into fields of vegetables or fruit unless there is a clear path or right of way, and keep to the path.

Ground-nesting birds
• During the breeding season (April-July) keep your dog on a lead or close at heel in areas such as moorland, forests, grasslands and the sea shore to avoid disturbing birds that nest on or near the ground.

Dog waste
• Always pick up dog faeces and dispose of properly.

Dog-friendly code
• Some people are nervous around dogs so consider their feelings.
• Keep your dog under control in public places.
• Never let your dog climb on furniture unless the owner has agreed this is acceptable.
• Don't leave your dog alone in a property unless you have the owner's agreement.

Wild camping
Wild camping is the only kind of camping allowed outside of designated campsites. When camping, any barbeques and fires must not be lit when a high fire threat has been declared. All fires must be kept under observation at all times.

Never light fires in green spaces or under tree canopy. Never cut green wood for burning for two reasons:
A It doesn't burn without producing a lot of smoke.
B It is a destruction of the natural habitat, such as fauna and local rare flower species like orchids.
Only light fires in places such as on beaches or a lochside near a water source where it will not disturb wildlife, and the smoke will not affect others. Extinguish any remnants before departing and clear the area. Never leave any rubbish or waste – take all litter and waste away with you. Many forestry sites have picnic and barbeque areas and facilities.

More information
outdooraccess-scotland.scot
forestryandland.gov.scot
nature.scot

walks

Pack his or her teddy and head to Scotland – many walks and adventures adjacent to the NC500…

Hebrides p44

On guard

Wild camping p64

A taste of North Scotland's finest circular dog walks for canines & their humans

Don't miss: Dog Walks - South Scotland too

Any biscuits eh?

Camera needed to capture your best buddy & you…

I love jumpers

Always pack a woolly

Kinloch Castle in Rum p80

Kyle of Tongue

The ultimate Scottish road trip, our route takes in the dramatic north west section of Assynt-Coigach in Sutherland and across the top of Scotland, with many awesome gems along the way.

Tongue you say?

The slipway on the Kyle of Tongue, with Ben Loyal behind

Caisteal Bharraich

1 At the Kyle of Tongue on the north coast is Ben Loyal, known as the 'Queen of Scottish Hills'. For a gentle walk and expansive views, walk from the village of Tongue to the remains of Caisteal Bharraich. The views north across the Kyle to Ben Hope and south to Ben Loyal are wonderful on a fine day.

Park in the village of Tongue. From the Kyle of Tongue hotel, turn left and left again onto a path next to a row of houses and follow the path behind them. Cross the footbridge and follow the path alongside the river before ascending to the diminutive castle ruin.

Tongue. 3km linear route. 30mins-1hr.

Kyle of Tongue

Tongue

P

Caisteal Bharraich

Cape Wrath

Balnakeil & Durness

4

Farr

Scrabster

John o' Groats

CAITHNESS

Loch Eriboll

5

Betty Hill

Tongue

1

SUTHERLAND

Ben Loyal

Wick

Scourie

Kylesku

Lochinver

Ardvreck Castle

3

Loch Shin

ASSYNT-COIGACH

Berriedale

10km
6m

Ullapool

Brora

Oldshoremore

Sutherland has some of mainland Scotland's finest and largely deserted beaches, backed by the mountains of Foinaven and Arkle, making for the wildest dog walks. For a more strenuous and remote route head to Sandwood Bay (see p52).

2 From the A383 at Rhiconich, at the head of Loch Inchard, turn left onto the B801 to Kinlochbervie. Before reaching the major fishing harbour turn right to Oldshoremore.

After 3km turn left into the hamlet of Oldshoremore. Drive down the steep and rugged road to the car park next to the cemetery (popular with campervans due to the proximity to the NC500 as there are facilities with fresh water). Access to the beach is the path from behind the car park to the wooden steps descending through the dunes and onto the broad pale sandy beach. At the far end and at low tide it's possible to cross the headland to the hamlet of Polin. At the far end of Polin beach is a path up onto the headland to enjoy the return views from a wooden bench.

The shallow beach is perfect for dogs, especially at low tide. The cliffs behind the beach are a geologists' dream too. Experts travel from far to study the rocks here – known as the Moine Thrust, featuring pink and black swirling shapes. The beaches are part of the Cape Wrath trail so keep an eye out for weary walkers and wild campers.
Oldshoremore-Polin. 5km. 2-3hrs.

Cape Wrath

Farr

John o' Groat

Betty Hill

CAITHNESS

2

Tongue

Kinlochbervie

Wick

SUTHERLAND

Kylesku

Ardvreck Castle

Loch Shin

Lochinver

ASSYNT-COIGACH

10km
6m

Hide 'n' seek

Exploring the rare rocks

Oldshoremore beach

NC500 | TIME: 30MINS-1HR | DISTANCE: 3KM/1¾M

Polin

Sunset in Polin

There is further parking in the next hamlet along the coast at Polin if the tide prevents the walk around the headland from Oldshoremore. The beach is accessed via the 'mermaid gate', descending the grassy headland to the small sandy beach. At the far end is a path ascent onto the headland – Am Meall – where there is a bench and fine return views.

Polin-Am Meall. 3km linear route. 1hr. ▶

Am
Meall

Polin
P

2
P Oldshoremore

Polin and Oldshoremore
from Am Meall headland

Gate to Polin beach

View from Polin Croft
holiday cottage

Don't miss! Ardvreck Castle, Smoo Cave, Loch Eriboll and Torrisdale Bay at Betty Hill. Plus more great beaches at Balnakeil, Farr, Armadale and Strathy…

3 **Ardvreck Castle** in Assynt sits on the banks of Loch Assynt, and the lochside shingle is a great spot to stretch the legs. The ruined castle dates from the 16th century alongside Calda House ruins, which dates from the 1700s. There is a visitor car park on A837, 3km north west of the village of Inchnadamph.

4 **Kyle of Durness and Smoo Cave.** North of Rhiconich the NC500 becomes single carriageway with passing places. Just before Durness is Balnakeil Bay, a peninsula that juts out into the North Sea. To the east of Durness is the intriguingly named Smoo Cave, a natural sea cave. The name originates from the Norse 'smjugg' or 'smuga', meaning a hole or hiding place. The sheltered estuary is where Norse sea farers moored their longboats. The cave chamber is very impressive - 15m high, 40m wide and 61m long. Inside the cave there is a path to a magnificent freshwater waterfall that falls 25 metres into an 8 metre deep pool. **Circular walk. Start/finishes at the car park.** ➤

5 **Loch Eriboll** offers a stunning drive on a ribbon of tarmac through the limestone landscape to access the very top of Scotland to the Kyle of Tongue and beyond.

The NC500 route takes in dramatic scenery

Ardvreck Castle
and Loch Assynt

Kylesku

North of Ardvreck castle is Kylesku, straddling two sea lochs. The hotel here is very dog-friendly. In a fantastic position just feet from the slipway, the seafood is as fresh as it's possible to be, as it comes off the key and straight into the kitchen - a fish lover's paradise. It is family-run and very relaxed and friendly - even the dogs are offered sausage for breakfast.

Local walks along the banks of Loch Glendhu and Loch Glencoul are from the doorstep, passing a huge water fall. The Glendhu Bothy sits on the lochside at the opposing end of the loch from the Kylesku. The hotel will send a rib to come and fetch you from Glendhu jetty after a wild night out in the Glendhu Bothy. Afterwards, treat yourself to a stay in the hotel in luxury. **9km linear undulating lochside track. 3 hours ●**

Sunrise at Loch Glendhu:
view from Kylesku Hotel

FACT FILE

Start/finish Inchnadamph-Kylesku-Durness-Tongue
Get there NC500; A894, 50km north west of Ullapool
Parking Free throughout
Time Take your time!
Terrain Kissing gates. One cattle grid and well maintained paths
Facilities Many car parks have a freshwater tap. Kinlochbervie has a Spar store. Fuel at Ullapool, Durness

Maps Landranger (1:50) 9, 10, 15
Dog advice Exposed cliff-top paths in places. Always check the tide times
Stay Kylesku Hotel is dog-friendly. Excellent restaurant, on-site walk around the hotel; kyleskuhotel.co.uk Polin Croft, Polin. Sleeps two; polinbeach.com
northcoast500.com
mountainbothies.org.uk

Glendhu Bothy

Loch Morlich

Enjoy a walk in the heart of Scotland among beautiful woodland in the historic Glenmore Forest National Park. There's no better way to explore the limitless landscape of the Cairngorm than from the lofty position of a campervan - with many hire centres to choose from, allowing you to make the most of your freedom to roam.

Chocks away!

Van with a view

1 From the Glenmore Visitor Centre, cross the road towards the Camping and Caravanning campsite. Head towards the pine forest and pick up the trail on Loch Morlich beach.

2 Follow the trail heading south. It is waymarked 'Loch Morlich Trail' with red indicators. The well-marked paths literally circuit the loch for 6km.

3 After 4km you will reach the 'The Old Logging Road'. Take care crossing before picking up the path on the far side that returns to the visitor car park. ● ➤

Glenmore Forest Park

The Queen's Forest

Loch Morlich

Rothiemurchus

We have lift off!
Bertie over Loch Morlich

FACT FILE

Start/finish NH976097
Distance 6km (3¾ miles)
Ascent 72m
Time 2 hours
Get there Take the Aviemore turning off the A9 onto the A905. In Aviemore, at the roundabout, take the turning 'The Cairngorm' B970 The Old Logging Way for 7km

Parking The visitor centre car park is opposite the Camping and Caravanning Site. There's a charge
Facilities, food & drink Visitor centre. Shop at the camp site
Terrain Mainly level, well-signed 'Loch Morlich Trail' paths throughout. Two road crossings
Maps OS Explorer (1:25) 57

Landranger (1:50) 36
Dog advice The route lies in an upland position of over 300m, surrounded by mountains. The weather can change very quickly, even in summer, so take extra layers
Stay Camping in the forest next to the loch is perfect; campingintheforest.co.uk

Spacious camping
among Glenmore forest
overlooking Loch Morlich

Black Water

An aptly named tumbling river, forest and falls that's easily accessible from Inverness, this is an ideal destination en-route to the NC500. A wealth of facilities and attractions are close by too, including grizzly bears...

The River Black Water flows from the hills and forest in Strathvaich south east to join the rivers Glascarnoch and Conon in the south, culminating at the location of the popular Falls of Rogie. This dramatic beauty spot is very busy all year round. However, nearby are the much quieter and spacious walking areas of the Black Water, Tor Breac and Strathgarve forest trails.

This is a spectacular area to visit, especially in late summer or autumn with abundant wildlife, colourful and rare funghi, as well as purple heather intertwined by the atmospheric and rugged River Black Water.

From the main A835 road north west of Inverness you will come to Contin, where there is a campsite and forestry area complete with carved Grizzly Bears. Rogie Falls is a little further on after Contin. Two kilometres after the town of Garve, passing over the railway level crossing, is Little Garve, signposted on your right hand side.

❶ At the far end of the car park is an old stone bridge. Cross here and turn left. Follow the riverside path for 2km, passing waterfalls and picnic areas to Silverbridge where there is a second stone bridge.

❷ At the Silverbridge bed and breakfast, cross the second bridge to take the return path on the opposing bank. Or, to extend the walk, turn right from the river to a more elevated forest section (Tor Beithe) which emerges at Home Farm before turning right on a track returning to Little Garve. ● ➤

Ceum Path

◀ Drochaid an Airgid
Silverbridge 1.5 km

Ceum Path

Gairbh ▶
Garve 1 km

**The riverside path
at Little Garve**

Silverbridge

A835

Torr
Bereac

Torr
Beithe

Home
Farm

Garve

FACT FILE

Start/finish NH395629
Distance 4km (2½ miles)
Get there Take the A835 and, 2km after Garve, look out for Little Garve Forestry. Turn on to the minor road. After half a mile you will see a sign to the left and a picnic area and bridge crossing the river
Parking Forestry, free
Time 1-2 hours
Terrain Well-maintained

riverside and woodland paths on both sides of Black Water
Facilities In car park, including a freshwater tap
Public services
Train and bus services from Inverness to Garve
Food & drink
Packed lunch recommended. Pub and Co-op at Strathpeffer
Maps OS Explorer (1:25) 437

Landranger (1:50) 20
Dog advice Fast running water and waterfalls in places
Stay Hotel in Garve. Camping in Contin. Silverbridge Bothy and B&B next to the river, with woodland and riverside walks from the door. airbnb.co.uk
forestryandland.gov.scot

Berriedale

This village on the north east coast between Helmsdale and Lybster overlooks a beautiful cove known as The Shore. The bay is sheltered by high rocky cliffs and is a favourite with birds and seals.

Exploring the rocky
northern section of The Shore

To Lybster

Moray Firth

Berriedale

3

P

1

The Shore

2

A9

P

To Helmsdale

There are two towers on the
cliff-top overlooking The Shore:
the remnants of a former castle

1 **The Shore Walk.** Turn off the A9 at Berriedale onto a minor road into an area of estate cottages and workshops. Park in the layby on the left. Walk past a row of four terraced cottages, keeping the burn on your left. Cross a suspended wire bridge over Berriedale Water and onto a sheltered cove surrounded by high cliffs. On the beach is a group of fishing cottages, two of which you can rent for short breaks or holidays. Exploring along the 500m beach reveals a vintage fishing winch and caves to explore.

2 **Berriedale Forts.** Off the sharp bend on the A9 walk into a yard to reveal a grassy path ascending the cliff top to the two historical forts: once part of the now-ruined Berriedale Castle. The views to The Shore below and along the coast are excellent. Keep dogs on a lead in wet and windy weather as there are no railings on the cliff edge. **Distance: 2km (1¼ miles).**

3 **Langwell Forestry.** A circular route alongside Langwell Water. Cross the A9 at Berriedale to join a forestry track. Cross the bridge over Langwell Water to a sporting estate. Turn sharp right to join a walled track back through an elevated section of the wood before descending back to the main road. **Distance: 4km (2½miles).** ●　　➤

Proper paw by paw terrain!

The Shore at Berriedale, with cliff-top forts in the distance

FACT FILE

Start/finish ND118227
Distance 500m - 4km (2½ miles)
Height/ascent 100m/150m
Get there Off the A9, 14km/8½ miles north of Helmsdale
Parking Free
Time 30min - 2hr short walks
Terrain One suspension bridge, pebbled beach, forest paths
Facilities None

Public services None
Food & drink Helmsdale
Maps OS Explorer (1:25) 444 Landranger (1:50) 17
Dog advice Exposed cliff-top paths at NCD119223, caution advised in wet, windy weather. Dogs best kept on harness and leash
Stay Two of the cottages at The Shore are owned and maintained by

The Landmark Trust and available for short breaks and holidays. The Shore is reached by a planked wire bridge which straddles Langwell and Berriedale Water. A pebbled beach is on your doorstep for exploring – the ultimate treat for your best friend; landmarktrust.org.uk

Elgol

Situated on the southern tip of the Strathaird Peninsula and reached by a dramatic drive around Loch Slapin, Elgol is a small fishing port offering dramatic views across to the Cuillin range from the shores of Loch Scavaig. The Camasunary Trail gives a taste of walking in the Cuillin Mountains without having to climb.

Bertie photo-bombing the Cuillin on the shores of Loch Scavaig

1 The start of the Camasunary Trail is 5km before Elgol on the B8083 from Broadford. The car park is next to the road, 500m after Kilmarie. Cross the road and pass through the gate to a John Muir Trust 'Strathaird' information board. The route is clear ahead of you - a gradual climb on a rough rocky path.

2 The route drops down to meet a river and a small waterfall. Our walk took place after a day of heavy rain, so the going was wet and muddy in places.

3 The path climbs gradually again, passing a small cairn on the left to reach an exposed slab of rock - Am Màm. The views across to the Cuillin are breathtaking; your eye is drawn to the unmistakable jagged peak of Sgùrr nan Gillean. Below, the sandy beach of Camasunary Bay is now clearly visible. The coastal views are widely regarded as some of the finest in Scotland, taking in the Isle of Rum across Loch Scavaig.

4 From here the path descends to the west past a waterfall, before descending more steeply. Continue on the track, which zig-zags until you cross the bridge over the river, reaching a green pasture at the east side of the bay. The small but very rugged peak of Sgurr na Stri is behind. Follow the boggy path to the relocated Camasunary bothy. Built to replace a former bothy across the bay, it's maintained by volunteers from the Mountain Bothy Association. An ideal place to stop and make a brew in poor weather.

5 Either re-trace your steps back to the information board and car park - a total of 9km. Alternatively, from the bay, pick up the path heading south from the footbridge you crossed earlier. The path skirts the peninsula, keeping Loch Scavaig on your right to Elgol for a total of 10km. Take care as the path is steep in places. Leave a second car at Elgol to return along the road to your (original) car at the start of the walk earlier. ● ➤

The descent from Am Màm

The view from the
Camasunary Trail
at Am Màm

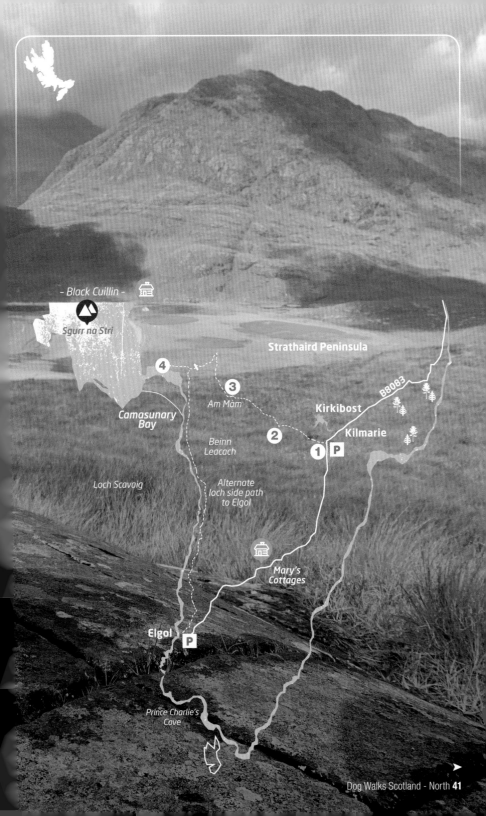

- Black Cuillin -

Sguir na Stri

Strathaird Peninsula

B8083

④

③

Am Màm

Kirkibost

Kilmarie

②

① P

Camasunary
Bay

Beinn
Leacach

Loch Scavaig

Alternate
loch side path
to Elgol

Mary's
Cottages

Elgol P

Prince Charlie's
Cave

Stunning rock formations
are worth exploring at Elgol

Tigh Mairi in Elgol is a dog-friendly traditional croft

FACT FILE

Start/finish NG545171
Distance 9km (5½ miles)
Height/ascent 198m/385m
Get there Cross the Skye Bridge at Kyle of Lochalsh, at the roundabout turn right to Broadford. In Broadford turn left onto the B8083. Car park on left side of B8083, 500m from Kilmarie, or 5km from Elgol

Parking Free (donation)
Time 3hrs
Terrain Rough, rocky uneven path
Facilities None
Public services Broadford has a Co-op store & fuel
Food & drink Own pack-up recommended
Maps OS Explorer (1:25) 411 Landranger (1:50) 32

Dog advice The Camasunary Estate is maintained by the John Muir Trust; johnmuirtrust.org mountainbothies.org.uk
Stay Authentic croft, dog-friendly, with mod cons. Sleeps four. Mary's Cottages; skyecottages.co.uk

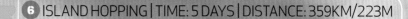

Hebrides

Make the most of the longest days of the year, traversing the Hebridean Way under the enormous skies of Scotland's Atlantic edge. Rich in heritage, Norse tales, miles of deserted white beaches and turquoise waters.

Let's go wild...

The first night, camping in the quiet dunes on Vatersay

For a Hebridean island hopping adventure you can pre-book your 'Hopscotch' ticket with Calmac Ferries allowing you to travel once, in either direction, between Oban and Castlebay on Barra, and return from Stornoway on Lewis to Ullapool. Most people make the trip from south to north, however either way is permissible. The islands' itinerary include Barra, Vatersay, Uist, Harris and Lewis.

1 Vatersay: on arriving at Castlebay, most visitors head north. Instead, drive south, crossing the causeway onto the island of Vatersay. Follow the Hebridean Way for 9km. At the narrowest stretch of road with dunes either side there is an extensive parking area for wild camping, including direct access onto 2km of pale sandy beach. It's an ideal spot for an overnight camp following a six-hour ferry crossing from Oban.

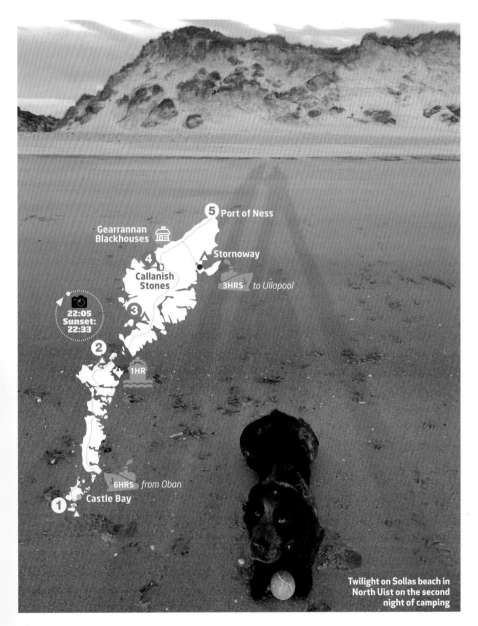

Twilight on Sollas beach in
North Uist on the second
night of camping

2 **Barra:** from the north coast of Barra, the short ferry crossing to Eriskay takes 40 minutes. Following the Hebridean Way, cross another causeway onto South Uist. Look out for huge whalebones next to a row cottages.

South Uist: this is a much flatter landscape compared to its neighbours. The road north is punctuated by hundreds of lochans, many of them decorated with dozens of water lilies.

North Uist: a visit to the well-known Benbecula Airport is a must, with its sand runway. Continue onto North Uist for 40km. At Grenitote, turn onto a minor road towards Sollas beach on the west coast. Here is a layby and picnic area - an ideal spot for a second night's camping behind the wild Atlantic beach (above). The walk across the dunes to the expansive beach is an ideal base for the summer solstice. ➤

3 **Harris:** from Sollas head for Berneray, a 15km drive away, to catch the next leg of the Hopscotch ferry service. It's a one-hour crossing to Leverburgh on the Isle of Harris. Here is probably the most famous beach in the Hebrides. Luskentyre is an outstanding white shell beach for 8km around a headland in the south west of Harris, with views across to Taransay. Look out for starfish! Behind the beach is a layby large enough for two campers and a couple of tents, with an honesty charge maintained by the West Harris Trust.

Lochans in South Uist

A Blackhouse in North Uist

Luskentyre beach
south west Harris,
third night's camp

4 Lewis: from Luskentyre head for Tarbert. It's perfect for stocking up on essentials at the Co-op store and Tarbert Stores where, like many, the proprietor speaks Gaelic. They sell barbeque fuel, candles and an array of camping gear. In town is also the Harris Tweed mill. From Tarbert head north on the A859 and onto the Isle of Lewis, home to the incredible Callanish Stone Circle and visitor centre on the A858 on the west coast. There are three main sites for a circular walk. **Distance: 3.5km/2m. Time: 1-2 hours; callanishvisitorcentre.co.uk**

5 Port of Ness and Stornoway: to complete the adventure and the traverse of the Hebrides, head for the Port of Ness, a fishing harbour on the far north coast. The final leg concludes in the capital town of Stornoway on the east coast. Nearby Laxdale campsite is perfectly positioned for a final night's camping before catching the ferry and the three-hour sailing to Ullapool on the mainland. It's a comfortable crossing, complete with restaurant and seating areas. The views on the approaches to the mainland are awesome. ●

Gearrannan Blackhouses

Tarbert Stores

Port of Ness

The Callanish Standing Stones date from 4,000 years ago

FACT FILE

Start/finish
NL665981/NB419326
Distance 359km (223 miles)
Get there Ferry: calmac.co.uk
Parking/camping
Free throughout. In Luskentyre, Harris there's a charge. Camping at the Talla na Mara estate includes three pitches with electric hook-up, water and waste facilities, showers. Seven further un-serviced pitches

Time 5 days/4 nights
Terrain Coastal, rugged terrain on Harris and Lewis
Facilities Castle Bay, Tarbert and Stornoway
Public services Public washrooms and showers at the larger ferry terminals
Food & drink
Own food and drink essential to start the trip

Maps OS Explorer (1:25) 452, 453, 454, 455, 456, 458, 459, 460
Landranger (1:50) 31, 22, 18, 14, 13, 8
Midges Be prepared in summer, take suitable repellent
Dog advice On Calmac Ferry services your dog must not be left alone in the car during the crossing.
westharristrust.org
tallanamara.co.uk
callanishvisitorcentre.co.uk

Solstice at Sollas

Starfish on Luskentyre

Camp cooking on a wood stove

Sandwood Bay

No trip to north west Sutherland is complete without a visit to Britain's wildest beach. Part of the Cape Wrath Trail, it's a long but reasonably flat walk. Huge dunes contain more than 200 different species of plants, including eight orchids, while Torridonian gritstone cliffs guard the beach from the southern approaches.

Off The Beaten Track

The approach to the beach is across the enormous dunes

Sandwood
Bay

Am Buachaille

*Sandwood
Loch*

④ *Loch Clais
nan Coinneal*

③

②

P ① **Blairmore**

Polin

Oldshoremore

1 Sandwood Bay car park at Blairmore is signposted from the main road, and the start of the route is opposite. Pass through a kissing gate next to a stone cottage, signed 'Sandwood 4½ miles'. Follow the path north on a gentle ascent with Loch Aisir on your right.

2 With Loch na Gainimh on your left the path forks. Keep left, following a northerly direction. From here the path crests a hill to reveal the route winding ahead of you - and a view of the cliff tops of Carn an Righ and Druim na Buainn away in the distance.

3 Just above a tiny lochan you'll see a pair of bicycle racks where the path narrows and becomes a little more rugged. The path gently undulates and you can see the highest points of the clifftops in front of you. The route is straightforward from here. Eventually the full scale of the beach is revealed when you reach gorse either side of the path and the ruin of Sandwood House in the valley below.

4 For an alternative and lofty approach to the bay, look out for a faint path on your left at 90 degrees with the southerly edge of Loch Clais nan Coinneal. A heathery route heads uphill between Carn an Righ and Druim na Buainn. The cliff tops offer broad views and a photo opportunity among the cotton grass. To gain your first view of Am Buachaille sea stack (The Shepherd), you will need to drop down across the grassy heathery moorland in a north westerly direction.

The return to the car park is via the main path from behind the dunes. Do take a pack-up and refreshments with you to make the most of your time on the beach. ● ➤

Shore-footed at
Sandwood Loch

Bike racks half way
along the route

Loch na Gainimh

Sandwood from the cliff-top
route at Druim na Buainn

A popular stop on
the Cape Wrath Trail

The cliff-top route affords lofty views of the bay and The Shepherd – Am Buachaille

FACT FILE

Start/finish NC194601
Distance 15km (9½ miles)
Height/ascent 131m/300m
Time 5 hours
Get there Car park on left side of road at Blairmore, signposted
Parking Free (donation)
Terrain One kissing gate at the start and one cattle grid. Well maintained path throughout
Facilities At start in car park, including freshwater tap
Public services Kinlochbervie has a Spar store
Food & drink Packed lunch recommended
Maps OS Explorer (1:25) 446 Landranger (1:50) 9
Maps This route is part of the Cape Wrath Trail; in summer you'll see wild campers on the beach
Dog advice Exposed cliff-top paths at NC205651. Caution advised in wet, windy weather. Dogs best kept on harness and leash. The Sandwood estate is maintained by the John Muir Trust and lies within a Special Area of Conservation; johnmuirtrust.org

Stac Pollaidh

Scotland's most popular mountain walk for good reason, this circular route offers views toward Assynt and the isolated mountains of Suilven and Canisp to the north, with the Summer Isles and Achiltibuie to the south west.

The views north to Assynt and Suilven

1 From the car park, cross the road, pass through the wooden gate and follow the stepped path next to the burn. After 100m the path flattens out at a junction of paths - take the left option. Most walkers take the right fork, but the left path is quieter and the fantastic views behind Stac Pollaidh are revealed in a more dramatic fashion, rewarding your efforts.

2 Follow the path on a steady ascent for 750m to large boulders on your left - a good spot for a breather and refreshments while taking in the south westerly views.

3 At 2km you will reach the top of the path and the north side of Stac Pollaidh. The views are spectacular north towards Suilven, Canisp and Cùl Mòr. This point is half way on the circular walk.

⊖ The steep path to the right is access to the airy summit - this is **not** recommended for dog walkers. Only experienced walkers with the appropriate equipment should tackle the summit. Continue on the lower path around the north side before gradually heading east and south with further spectacular views of Loch Lurgainn and Ben Mor Coigach. ● ➤

Stac Pollaidh from
the junction of paths

The descent from Loch Lurgainn with Cùl Beag on the left

The north side of Stac, Suilven Canisp and Loch Sionascaig

FACT FILE

Start/finish NC107095
Distance 4km (2½ miles)
Height/ascent 500m/420m
Get there A835 from Ullapool, after 14km turn left onto minor road. Car park on left after 8km: IV26 2YB
Parking Pay & display
Time 2-3 hours
Terrain One gate at the start. Well maintained path throughout

Facilities None
Public services Bus service from Ullapool
Food & drink Packed lunch recommended
Maps OS Explorer (1:25) 439 Landranger (1:50) 15
Dog advice Keep to the lower circular path at NC110106. The elevated path on the north side

to the summit is for experienced walkers only. Not suitable for dogs. This is a very popular route so pick your visit times outside of weekends if possible
Stay Campsite at Ardmair on the banks of Loch Kanaird; ardmair.com

Wild Camping

Scotland offers idyllic wild camping, with many remote and open spaces beside the coast, island lochs and mountains. Nothing fills the senses more than a wild night out or two - and it's a hugely exciting adventure for your dog too.

Gruinard Bay

MAKING CAMP

There's something so exciting and connecting about camping out with your dog in tow. For your best friend, as soon as the nylon fly sheet becomes a three dimensional shape complete with 'front door' it becomes a home for his or her pack - to be guarded at all costs! It can be a difficult choice for your hound whether to tear along the beach or keep watch of the guy ropes. It's a canine paradox: one which they inevitably attempt to do all at once of course, as well as keeping a keen eye on the food, camp fire and stove situation. After all, it's five o'clock somewhere, whether their bowl is at home or on the road, such is the creature of habit. They instinctively know when dinner time is...

Setting up camp is a hugely poignant and sensory experience as the setting sun cloaks the small and remote beach to the north of Torridon in warm shades of amber, and we watch a hearty stew bubbling away on the stove. As the deepening glow disappears behind Gruinard Island a haar swirls in across the horizon like a veil, replacing the orange glow with shades of blue – the colour of night. While the towering mountain of An Teallach stands guard behind, as it always has for centuries.

Our sparkling libation is cooling in the lap of the bay on the receding tide.

The combination of shifting landscape, food and drink is like a cosy hug (from the Old Norse 'hugga', meaning to comfort) before snuggling

down into my sleeping bag, with the familiar warmth of Spaniel in the small of my back. The only sound to accompany us tonight will be the distant gentle lapping of water along the bay, becoming louder towards dawn on the incoming tide. Apart from my companion's tent a few metres away, we are alone.

In a matter of hours, we wake to a breathtaking sunrise, drink tea and then run along the beach, splashing along in the autumn water before heading along the road of discovery once more.

Wild camping is a way of life in a Scottish summer and is perfectly legal and acceptable, provided you adhere to the Scottish Outdoor Access Code and Camping Code of Conduct, of course (see p12). ➤

Canine Cocktails

Seaside Flysheet Toddy

This features smoky Islay Scotch and earthy tones of Genièvre (juniper) syrup.
- Dash of Islay whisky
- Slug of Genièvre syrup
- Splash of cranberry juice
- Half a mug of hot water

Combine the Scotch, syrup and cranberry juice and stir together over a fire or stove.

Genièvre syrup:
- Half a cup of hot water
- Half a cup of honey
- Two Earl Grey tea bags

Mix together the hot water and honey. Add tea bags and allow to steep for five minutes.

Salty Dog

A coastal camp favourite, the combination of sun and salt is synonymous with the coast.
- Splash of grapefruit juice
- Slug of vodka or gin
- Pinch of salt

Salt the rim of a glass. Shake inside a hip flask and serve.

Dirty Dog Cocktail

- Slug of cognac
- Shot of vodka
- Slug of orange juice
- Slug of cranberry juice

Combine ingredients in a water bottle or hip flask.

Fuzzy Dog

- Dash of peach schnapps
- Shot of Amaretto almond liqueur
- Generous splash of coconut rum
- Orange juice

Add ingredients into your bidon and cool in the surf before serving. Forage small pebbles from the beach for ice cubes.

Sunset over Gruinard island

CAMP COOKING

Cooking outdoors over a wood fire is one of the most fun and rewarding experiences. Combined with fresh air, the end result tastes amazing too...

Packing for your camp kitchen

- Water bottles filled with fresh water
- Filter water bottle
- Camping gas and portable stove
- A small chopping board
- Folding pocket knife
- A wooden spoon and Sporks
- Clean bamboo canes (for bread sticks)
- First aid kit

Camping gas stoves are the simplest and easiest way to cook up a quick meal. A Dutch tripod oven may not be practical when travelling. However, if you can find sufficient dry wood and you have a safe location, a real fire is an unbeatable cooking experience, as well as keeping you warm as the evening sun sets. An old Boy Scout's trick is to make pre-prepared food at home before wrapping in foil, and simply bake using a real fire.

Making a wood fire

When gathering wood for a real fire, dead wood is ideal, so gather dry driftwood, bunches of pine needles, twigs and branches. Silver birch bark peeling and pine cones are nature's fire lighters. Never cut trees or use green wood as it simply doesn't burn - and will create a lot of smoke before it does.

Campfire Bread Sticks

Breadsticks baked over the fire - tasty and perfect for camping!

- 2 cups plain flour
- 2 teaspoons baking powder
- 5 tablespoons sugar
- 1 teaspoon salt
- ¼ cup olive oil
- ¾ cup water

Make ahead of your trip: mix the ingredients together, portion the dough into equally sized balls and wrap in foil. In camp, roll each ball into a rope - wrapping around a sturdy stick or cane is ideal. Rotate over the fire so the bread cooks evenly for five minutes.

Berry Melon Muffin Pud

A pudding mix placed inside half a melon skin with added seasonal fruits, jam or golden syrup and baked in the embers of a fire. Again make as many of these as desired at home before travelling.

- 2 oz butter
- 2 oz caster sugar
- 2 oz self raising flour
- 1 large egg, beaten
- 2 tablespoons milk
- 2 tablespoons of jam or syrup

Cream together the butter and sugar until smooth. Mix in the egg and milk gradually, so as not to curdle the butter. Sift the flour, fold in gently. For a flourish add 2 tablespoons of golden syrup, treacle or jam in bottom of skin before adding the batter. Try adding fresh berries to the top before wrapping the individual skins in foil and baking in the dying embers of your fire.

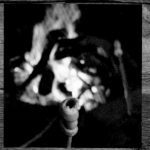

When it comes to camping equipment, what to take or leave behind can be a dilemma. Do you pack light or cover all bases and take all bar the kitchen sink?

Picking the right spot for a fire

Pay close attention to the ground before preparing any fire. Sand, rock or gravel are ideal bases with no tree canopy. Supervise young or energetic dogs around stoves or fires, and never build a fire on grass, machair or plants. Always distinguish a fire before departing and make the area as you found it.

If travelling light and for a small contained fire, look at a folding stove like the Vargo Hexagon Stove, which folds into a nylon sleeve and is super lightweight. A Kelly Kettle is a great piece of kit for plenty of hot water, although a simple camp kettle is perfect too. Primus make a cooking pan and bowl set. For the ultimate set-up the Tentipi and stove set is king. ● ➤

Vargo folding stove

Tripod stove

Loch side camping with a spacious Tentipi

Making the most of wet weather

Charlie in the dunes

Loch Ewe

Gruinard Island

Loch Broom

Ullapool

An Teallach

Loch Maree

Slioch

Loch Torridon

Liathach

Atmospheric sunset and haar combo

Pitch perfect

FACT FILE

Legality Wild camping is legal and acceptable thanks to the Land Reform (Scotland) Act 2003, which entitles you to camp on the majority of unenclosed land, provided you adhere to the Scottish Outdoor Access Code, see p12
Time Two to three nights with a hotel to finish is the ideal format!
Where Coastal areas away from homes, gardens and livestock.

Lochside areas are often made up of sand or shingle. Generally speaking the wilder the location the better for you and your dog. There are seasonal restrictions in Loch Lomond and the surrounding Trossachs during the summer
Food & drink
Own water, food and drink essential
 Advice In the height of summer midges and ticks

can present a nuisance, especially in humid and still conditions. Late spring (May/June) and early autumn (September) are the best months to avoid them. Always respect wildlife, and remove and bin **all** waste.
outdooraccess-scotland.scot
wildstoves.co.uk
finisterreuk.com primus.eu

Little Wyvis

Often, the smaller hills in Scotland afford stunning views to rival their bigger siblings - and the smaller of the two Wyvis' reward the walker with lofty views across to Torridon in the west and the Black Isle to the east.

I ♥ you

This route up Little Wyvis, a Corbett, is via the easier broad farm tracks above Silverbridge on the A835. The views are extensive to Black Isle and the Cromarty and Beauly Firth. Looking west are range upon range of mountains as far as Torridon, with the reservoirs of Loch Luichart and Loch Glascarnoch in the foreground.

1 From the car park at Silverbridge, cross the old bridge over the river Black Water. At Silverbridge B&B, follow the path to the left rounding a gate and a cattle grid. Follow the track through farm pasture, keeping a barn on your right. Keep dogs under close control as sheep and horses are grazing here.

2 At a line of pine trees, pass through a gate in a deer fence. Follow the winding trail now on a steeper incline. Note many rare mosses and lichens lining the path with purple heather during the summer months. At the first junction of paths, keep right, heading uphill. Your objective is straight above you at this stage of the climb.

3 At a second and third junction of paths keep left. Follow the stony path as it zig-zags uphill. The approach to the summit is from the right of the cairn. The summit is broad and fairly flat. Hunker behind the cairn to enjoy the views and some refreshments. The descent follows the same route to Silverbridge. ● ➤

The path above
Strathgarve Forest

Strathgarve Forest

Little Wyvis

1

P

2

3

A835

Black Water

Garve

Waiting for a reward on Little Wyvis summit

FACT FILE

Start/finish NH401639
Distance 10km (6 miles)
Height/ascent 763m/657m
Get there 3 miles after Garve on left hand side of A835 Silverbridge, Easter Ross: IV23 2PU
Parking Forestry, free
Time 3 hours
Terrain One cattle grid, farm gates. Farm tracks at lower level, heather-lined paths higher up

Facilities Toilets in car park
Public services Train and bus services from Inverness to Garve
Food & drink Pub and Co-op at Strathpeffer
Maps OS Explorer (1:25) 437 Landranger (1:50) 20
Advice Livestock and horses grazing on lower slopes above Silverbridge. Weather and temperatures can change and drop

dramatically at altitude, so always pack extra layers and a hat and gloves, even in summer
Stay Silverbridge Bothy, a retreat next to the river Black Water, and the Silverbridge B&B with covered veranda decking, hill and woodland walks from the door; airbnb.co.uk forestryandland.gov.scot

An edible Cep or Penny Bun

Isle of Rùm

From Mallaig, on the Road to the Isles, is Rùm on the west coast of Scotland. A National Nature Reserve, and home to a diverse range of wildlife, it's a stunning coastal landscape, with dramatic hills with Scandinavian names. Try an overnight bothy stay on the Atlantic coast for the ultimate trekking adventure.

Rùm has a small population – only around 35 people live here throughout the year in Kinloch, the only village. The island is owned by the Isle of Rùm Community Trust, who run and maintain the accommodation options, as well as the village shop and post office. Kinloch Castle is worth a visit too.

① For a trans-isle traverse from Kinloch to Guirdil Bay on the west coast, the trail from Kinloch is straight forward, while the second section is rough hillside, passing over Bealach a' Bhraigh Bhig, before dropping down into Glen Guirdil. Good navigation skills are required in poor weather. Our group of six employed a guide, taking enough food and fuel for an overnight stay in Guirdil bothy – nestled into the back of the bay looking out towards Canna. It's a great wild spot with a fresh water river nearby, where you have a good chance of

seeing both white-tailed sea eagles and golden eagles, as well as red deer and feral goats. During the summer, Guirdil is a magical place to watch the sunset, and in winter the northern lights are often seen during the dark nights, and are best during autumn and early spring. **20km linear route. 6 hours' walking. Overnight: Guirdil bothy** ➤

Pier on Loch Scresort

Kilmory

Glen Shellesder

Guirdil Bothy

① Kinloch Glen

Kinloch

To Mallaig

2HR

Loch Scresort

Isle of Rùm

Harris

② Hallival

Charlie having a ball
near Guirdil bothy

Loch
Scresort

Kinloch

Coire Dubh

cairn

Hallival

Coire nan
Grunnd

Loch Coire
nan Grunnd

For lofty views of the island, across to Skye and the Scottish mainland, take a hike from Kinloch to the summit of Hallival – a Corbett standing at 723m. The route takes in Atlantic Corrie, a rough and rugged traverse with some huge boulders in places requiring some easy scrambling.

2 From Kinloch village follow the path next to the stream along Allt Slugan a' Choillich towards the Dam and Coire Dubh for 3km. From the cairn at Bealach Bairc-Mheall follow the ridge to the summit of Hallival. To descend, head west down to Coire nan Grunnd to the loch. Pick up the path from the north east end of the loch and head north to return to Kinloch. 11km circular route. 4 hours' walking. Total ascent: 808m ●

Atlantic Corrie

Views to Cuillin on Skye

Start/finish NM401996
Get there CalMac Ferries from Mallaig to Kinloch: two hours
Parking None; car-free island
Time 4/6 hours' walking
Terrain Gravel tracks, loose, rough rocky paths
Food & drink Toilets, showers, tea shop, post office and bike hire
Maps OS Explorer (1:25) 397 Landranger (1:50) 39
Dog advice Wild deer roaming. The island can experience wild weather, even in summer, so make sure that you have suitable clothing and footwear as the roads and tracks are very rough and rocky in places
Stay In Kinloch there is a campsite, camping cabins, wild camping and the Harbour BBQ Hut; isleofrum.com
mountainbothies.org.uk

Kinloch Castle

A summit cairn on Hallival looking towards Atlantic Corrie and Glen Harris

Guirdil bothy

Cullen

Here's the lovely Bertie, sniffing out a section of the 75km Speyside Whisky Trail at Cullen Bay - famous for the delicious fish dish, Cullen Skink - followed by a whizz around The Windings...

1 Cullen: arriving at this distinctive coastal village you'll spot a huge overhead aqueduct and harbour alongside the broad beach. Pass under the aqueduct into the car park. Aim for low tide - the beach is popular with dog walkers, with several happy hounds belting across it. Rock lovers will enjoy the pink marble-like sea stacks known as The Three Kings. Following a good run along the sand, head east on the Moray Coast Trail across the footbridge into town, passing Seatown Harbour, designed by Thomas Telford.

Beyond Seatown, follow the minor road past Cullen Rowing Club, and then continue along the Moray Coastal Trail and past the remarkable Cullen Pet Cemetery. Run by a local volunteer for 20 years, even a washed-up porpoise lies here. Follow the coast track, which eventually becomes a grassy path. For a wilder coast walk head east to Logie Head, which is popular for climbing.

Beach: 3km linear route. 1 hour.
Moray Coastal Trail: 6km linear route. 2 hours.

Bow Fiddle Rock

Logie Head

P

A98

Seatown

Cullen

The rocky eastern
end of Cullen Bay

Fochabers

2 **The Windings,** as their name suggests, are a maze of trails through 19th century pine woodland and the gardens of the Duke and Duchess of Gordon. A choice of trails reveal all manner of wildlife - watch out for capercaillie and red squirrels. During autumn look out for several rare species of fungi, including the wonderfully named Orange Birch Bolete (a stunning mushroom), and the iconic toadstool, the Fly Agaric.
Trail: 2-5km circular routes. ●

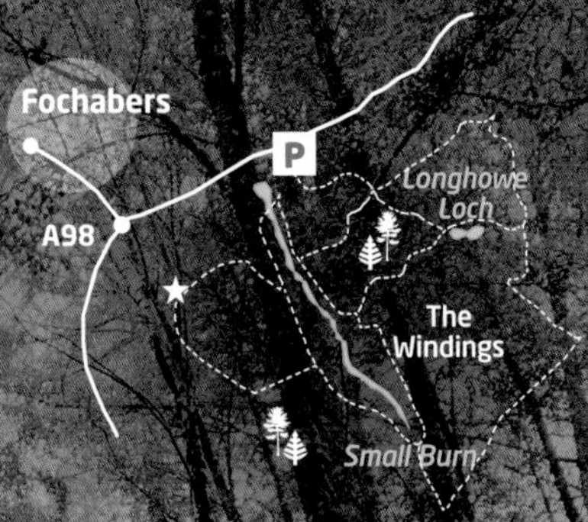

Fochabers

A98

P

Longhowe Loch

The Windings

Small Burn

Bertie stays alert for red squirrels at The Windings

Juno - a rare still moment

FACT FILE

Start/finish Cullen: NJ505673
Distance 3km (2 miles)
Height/ascent 0m/0m
Get there Car park under aqueduct at Cullen Links
Windings: IV32 7PG
Parking Cullen: free;
Windings: Pay & display
Time 1-3 hours
Terrain Sandy beach, coast path, forest trails. Several footbridges

Facilities Café at Cullen Links car park, including toilets
Public services
Regular bus services along Moray
Food & drink Seatown, Cullen; Fochabers has pubs and a Co-op
Maps OS Explorer (1:25) 424
Landranger (1:50) 28
Dog advice Check tide times
Stay Cluaran Chalet, Auchenhalrig, Fochabers IV32 7PP. Tucked away in

the heart of a rural hamlet. Enclosed garden, decking area; airbnb.com/h/cluaranchalet
Farm shop Lower Mill of Tynet organic farm along the track from Auchenhalrig has an automated shop for milk in reusable glass bottles, eggs and preserves; lowermilloftynet.co.uk

Orange Birch Bolete

Dawn in Auchenhalrig

Achiltibuie

Tucked away from the popular NC500 route, the Coigach peninsula offers stunning views across to the Summer Isles in the south and the unmistakable icons of Suilven and Stac Pollaidh to the north (see p60).

Off The Beaten Track ►

The deserted Achnahaird Bay backed by Suilven to the north

COIGACH

Achnahaird Bay

P
②

P

Loch Osgaig

Isle Ristol

Achiltibuie
①

Summer Isles

Horse Island

1 Step back in time on a trip to Achiltibuie - its pebble beach backed by a grassy meadow and strewn with historical marine buoys, abandoned boats and a collection of vintage anchors… proof time has stood still here. The views across to the Summer Isles are stunning.

The village lies within the Wester Ross National Scenic Area, the North West Highlands Geopark, the Wester Ross Biosphere Reserve and is a Marine Protected Area. Close to the village is a geology trail featuring a series of walks and providing an insight into the landscape.

The roads across the rocky landscape of Inverpolly are spectacular as they weave their way, threading together valleys, bays and moorland, passing the peaks of Cul Beag, Cùl Mòr and the sugar-loaf shape of Suilven. ➤

Achiltibuie, complete with marine curiosities

2 On the northern side of the Coigach peninsula is a deserted, expansive sandy beach and the dunes of Achnahaird Bay - ideal for a good safe run around and the chance to lose, or find, several balls. ●

Locholly Lodge features an elevated glass sitting area to take advantage of the views

FACT FILE

Start/finish Achnahaird:
NC015140; Achiltibuie: NC030075
Distance 3km (1¾ miles)
Get there Car park at end of
minor road. Signposted from A835,
16km north of Ullapool
Parking Free
Time 30 mins - 3 hours
Terrain Dunes, sandy beaches
and a pebble beach
Facilities None

Public services
Achiltibuie has an independent
general store and post office.
Ullapool has a supermarket and
is 16km (10 miles) away
Food & drink
Picnic lunch recommended
on a fine day
Maps OS Explorer (1:25) 439
Landranger (1:50) 15
Stay Locholly Lodge in Polglass

to the east of Achiltibuie general
stores. Features spacious, modern
accommodation with a hot tub on
decking overlooking the Summer
Isles. Locholly Lodge, Polglass
Achiltibuie, Wester Ross IV26 2YH
T: 07947 754454
greatselfcatering.com/
locholly-lodge

Maritime museum

Locholly Lodge has lofty views

Fairy Pools

At the foot of the Black Cuillin near Glenbrittle are the Fairy Pools. A cascade of crystal clear blue water make for a perfect Spaniel wild swim spot on the River Brittle, backed by a dramatic curtain of rock.

Carbost

P

Glenbrittle

- Black Cuillin -

River Brittle

Loch Brittle

Soay Sound

1 On the road to the Isle of Skye at Kyle of Lochalsh is the unmissable Eilean Donan Castle, situated on an island at the point where three sea lochs meet. An ideal place to stop en-route for the views and visitor centre.

The Fairy Pools, near Carbost on the west of Skye, are a series of cascading pools and waterfalls on the River Brittle. There are impressive views towards their source - the Black Cuillin. Glenbrittle is a magical place popular with walkers and wild swimmers.

Take some time to work your way up the river and explore all the pools and huge boulders.

The first waterfall is the highest fall with the deepest pool. On the other side of the river from the path it is possible to jump into the deep blue pool from 10 metres high. The second pool up is the most famous - a crystal clear blue pool featuring a natural arch beneath the water. Follow the main path up beside the river to take in more of the mountains. Return route is the same way. **2.4km linear route. 45 mins.**

Eilean Donan Castle, Kyle of Lochalsh

FACT FILE

Start/finish Coral Beach: NG232537. Fairy Pools: NG423258
Distance 2.4/4km (1½/2½ miles)
Get there Eilean Donan: IV40 8DX. **Fairy Pools:** Forestry Commission signposted 'Glumagan Na Sithichean' and 'Fairy Pools'. On the road that leads to Glenbrittle, 9km from Carbost. **Coral Beach:** at the end of the single track road, 7km from Dunvegan

Parking Free
Time 1-2 hours
Terrain Well used footpaths, rocky and sandy beaches
Facilities Kyle of Lochalsh Visitor Centre. Broadford has a Co-op store and fuel
Public services None
Maps OS Explorer (1:25) 407, 411

Landranger (1:50) 23, 32
Dog advice Take care near the fairy pools, deep water in places
Stay Authentic thatched stone crofts; dog-friendly with mod cons. Electronic gated gardens, sleep four. Mary's Cottages: skyecottages.co.uk

Coral Beach

2 Coral Beach is situated in the north of Skye adjacent to the small crofting community of Claigan, 7km north along a single track road from Dunvegan and the castle. Or, 41km (45 minutes) from Portree.

The beach is made of crushed red Coralline seaweed (also known as maërl) from a reef near the Isle of Lampay. Coralline grows very slowly at around 1mm per year. The sun-bleached white coral renders the water a stunning turquoise blue - perfect for water loving dogs and their human(s).

To reach it, aim for the far end of the car park and a kissing gate. Follow the fairly level, stony farm track off to the right. There are some stream crossings, all with stepping stones. Pass through another kissing gate. When you reach the first smaller bay the track divides. Take the left hand option. Head for a break in a stone wall. When you reach the top of the rise you will now get your first view of Coral Beach. Well worth a photograph.

The return is that same route back to the car park. **4km linear route. 1 hour.** ●

Lampay

Coral Beach

P
Claigan

Loch Dunvegan

Dunvegan Castle

Dunvegan

Loch Ness

For epic views head to Whitebridge, a hamlet roughly midway along the south side of Loch Ness, where it crosses the River Fechlin in the foothills of the Monadhliath Mountains in The Great Glen.

Whitebridge

P

General Wade's Military Road

River Fechlin

Sheep Pens

Beinn Sgurrach

The walk from the Whitebridge Hotel is ideal for twitching, with Goldcrests and Red Kites soaring. Here, Beinn Sgurrach peak is in the distance

Foyers

River Foyers

Dell Estate

Whitebridge

P

① Option one: Cross Whitebridge, passing through the riverside holiday lodge park. Go through the farm gate and follow the uphill track. There's plenty of high-pitched chatter among several clumps of dense pine as we ascend, and we spot a flock of Goldcrests feeding among the pine cones in the bright autumn sunshine. Beyond a quadrangle of sheepfold ruins is a gate, where it's possible to climb a further 200m to the summit of Beinn Sgurrach (470m) - an excellent viewpoint on a fine day. **5km linear route. 2 hrs. Ascent 266m.**

② Option two: Turn left opposite Whitebridge into 'Dell Estate'. Follow the track, keeping the River Fechlin and farm buildings on your right into open country before picking up the river again. Cross a ford through a wooded area to reach the junction with a minor road. Follow this north. There's a weir to your right. Cross the River Fechlin into the village, taking car of any passing cars. Opposite the Post Office is a kissing gate into the Falls. It winds steeply down to the viewing platforms.
12km linear route. 3-4 hrs. Ascent 270m. ➤

Whitebridge from the hills

Whitebridge over the Fechlin

Falls of Foyers

●Inverness

Loch Ness

Urquhart
Castle

●Foyers

Whitebridge

Fort ●
Augustus

On the south banks of Loch Ness.
There are many laybys and picnic
spots to enjoy on a fine day

3 **Option three:** Loch Ness is 22 miles long. There are several paths along the quieter south eastern side at Foyers Bay, Inverfarigaig and on the banks with views across to Urquhart Castle. The route is part General Wade's Military Road (B852). There are several parking spots and laybys, many with picnic benches and designated barbeque areas. Keep a look out for more wildlife, especially red squirrels. **Linear and circular routes from the loch banks through woodland.** ●

Start/finish NH487152
Distances 2/5/12km
Get there 25 miles south of Inverness on the B862 or 10 miles north of Fort Augustus
Parking Pay & display at Foyers
Time 1-3 hours
Terrain Riverside paths, upland farm tracks
Facilities Nearest at Foyers, St Augustus and Inverness
Public services None
Food & drink Whitebridge Hotel
Maps OS Explorer (1:25) 416 Landranger (1:50) 34, 35
Dog advice Livestock grazing. At Falls of Foyers, dogs must be kept on a lead throughout – dramatic sheer drops from the two fenced viewing platforms
Stay Whitebridge Hotel, Stratherrick IV2 6UN. Comfortable relaxed country house hotel; whitebridgehotel.co.uk

Speyside Way

The Speyside Way extension follows the arteries of old railway lines, passing through the heart of whisky country. In short, this trail is a must for those seeking a taste of the Highlands.

The Speyside Way Extension is a recent innovation to the original route that extends from Moray to Aviemore. The extension now connects this popular long-distance route to Kingussie and Newtonmore. It provides a way-marked trail route through Inshriach Forest with a mix of new paths and upgraded forestry tracks. From Insh, the existing off-road route (which follows the route of the Badenoch Way) continues past Inveruglass and the historic Ruthven Barracks.

1 Parking at Inshriach Forest car park. Well maintained forest trails throughout the forest, with some climbs to take in the extensive views across to the Monadhliath mountains. The circular forest trails feature regular picnic tables and benches for a relaxing and enjoyable few hours with your best four-legged friend. There are a choice of routes for a longer day out. Look out for wildlife such as raptors, red squirrels and wildfowl on Insh Marshes Nature Reserve. ●

A cairn in Inshriach Forest

The trail near Inveruglass

FACT FILE

Start/finish
NH835023/NH810007
Distance 4-8km (2½-5 miles)
Height/ascent 334m/120m
Get there Turn off the A9 at Kingussie onto the B970 to Ruthven Barracks and Old Milton. Pass through Insh to Loch Insh
Parking Free/pay & display
Time 1-3 hours
Terrain Forest paths and trails

Facilities At start in car park, including freshwater tap
Public services
Train from Edinburgh or Glasgow to Kingussie
Food & drink
Kingussie, Loch Insh Visitor Centre
Maps OS Explorer (1:25) 56, 57 Landranger (1:50) 35
Dog advice The Speyside Way is a shared use path for walkers,

cyclists and horse riders;
cairngorms.co.uk
lochinsh.com
Stay Kirkstone Lodge, Inveruglass. Sitting area with chaise longues overlooking the Monadhliath mountains, plus a woodburner, hot tub and enclosed garden;
kirkstonelodge.com

Kirkstone Lodge

SPEY
SPEYSIDE DISTILLERY

Modern comfort